WORKBOOK

5

**ENSINO FUNDAMENTAL
ANOS INICIAIS**

RENATO MENDES CURTO JÚNIOR
ANNA CAROLINA GUIMARÃES
CIBELE MENDES

CONTENTS

UNIT 1
Fun, hobbies, and games! _____ 3

UNIT 2
The seasons of the year _____ 6

UNIT 3
Different cities _____ 9

UNIT 4
Matt's family _____ 16

UNIT 5
Means of transportation _____ 18

UNIT 6
At the school cafeteria _____ 20

UNIT 7
A message to a friend _____ 27

UNIT 8
Traveling with friends _____ 30

UNIT 1
FUN, HOBBIES, AND GAMES!

1 What leisure activity is it?

a)

b) _____

c) _____

d) _____

_____

e)

f) _____

g) _____

h) _____

_____

2 Brainstorm activities you like and don't like doing! Examples: watching tv, reading books, playing soccer, etc. Then complete the table.

In my free time...	
I like	I don't like...

3 Now, write one or two sentences telling people what you like or don't like doing in your free time.

Pay attention:
* Use "and" to list the things you **like**.
* Use "or" to list the things you **don't like**.

Example

I like watching TV, playing games **and** reading books. But I don't like cleaning my room, talking on the phone **or** sleeping.

_____
_____
_____
_____
_____
_____
_____
_____

4 Complete the sentences with **am**, **is** or **are**.

a) _____ you hungry?

b) _____ Rachel tired?

c) Susan and Rick _____ confused.

d) You _____ sad.

e) She _____ not angry.

f) I _____ surprised.

g) _____ Caio scared of the movie?

h) _____ the dog happy?

UNIT 2 — THE SEASONS OF THE YEAR

1. Match the following items to the season they belong to.

a)

Autumn/fall

b)

Winter

c)

Spring

d)

Summer

2 What season of the year is it?

a)

	summer
	autumn/fall
	winter
	spring

c)

	summer
	autumn/fall
	winter
	spring

b)

	summer
	autumn/fall
	winter
	spring

d)

	summer
	autumn/fall
	winter
	spring

3 Read the weather forecast below and mark **T** (True) or **F** (False) for the statements about it.

☐ This is the weather forecast for Washington.

☐ There is a big difference in temperature between Saturday and Tuesday.

☐ It's sunny on Sunday.

☐ It's very cold on Monday.

UNIT 3
DIFFERENT CITIES

1 What place is it? Name each one of them.

a)

b)

c)

d)

e)

f)

g)

h)

2 Give the directions.

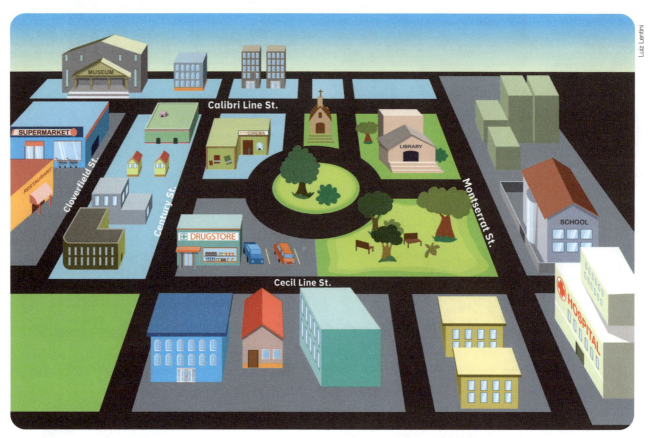

a) Go from the restaurant to the cinema.
_____
_____
_____
_____
_____

b) Go from the school to the Museum.
_____
_____
_____
_____
_____

3 Read these signs from a park.

CITY PARK

In this park we have:
- A kids' playground
- A picnic area
- A reading area
- A roller-skating rink
- A fishing pond
- A sand playground

Enjoy our park!

CITY PARK

Park rules:
- Dogs are not allowed!
- No bikes!
- Don't swim in the pond!
- Throw trash in the dumpsters!
- Don't climb the trees!

Enjoy our park!

4 What can kids do in this park? Mark in the sentences below.

a) Roller-skate ☐

b) Fish ☐

c) Walk their dogs ☐

d) Build sandcastles ☐

e) Climb trees ☐

f) Have a picnic ☐

g) Play ☐

h) Ride a bike ☐

i) Read a book ☐

j) Swim ☐

5 These signs represent some rules in the park. Complete the rules with these verbs: **swim**, **ride** and **take**.

a) Don't _____ bikes in the park!

b) Don't _____ your dogs to the park.

c) Don't _____ in the pond.

6 Use the following nouns to name the places represented in the pictures below.

> Restaurant • Hospital • Drugstore
> Supermarket • Library

a)
_____

b)
_____

c)
_____

d)
_____

e)
_____

7 Tick what you can find in your street or neighborhood.

a) ☐ Drugstore

b) ☐ Cinema

c) ☐ Supermarket

d) ☐ Post office

e) ☐ Police station

f) ☐ Bank

g) ☐ School

h) ☐ Bakery

i) ☐ Others: _____
_____

8 Complete. Where do we go when...

a)

... we are sick?

_____

_____

c)

... we want to buy food?

_____

_____

b)

... we want to buy clothes?

_____

_____

d)

... we want to buy bread?

_____

_____

UNIT 4
MATT'S FAMILY

1 Complete the family tree with the correct family member relationship.

2 Draw and color a picture of your family. You can include anyone you consider family.

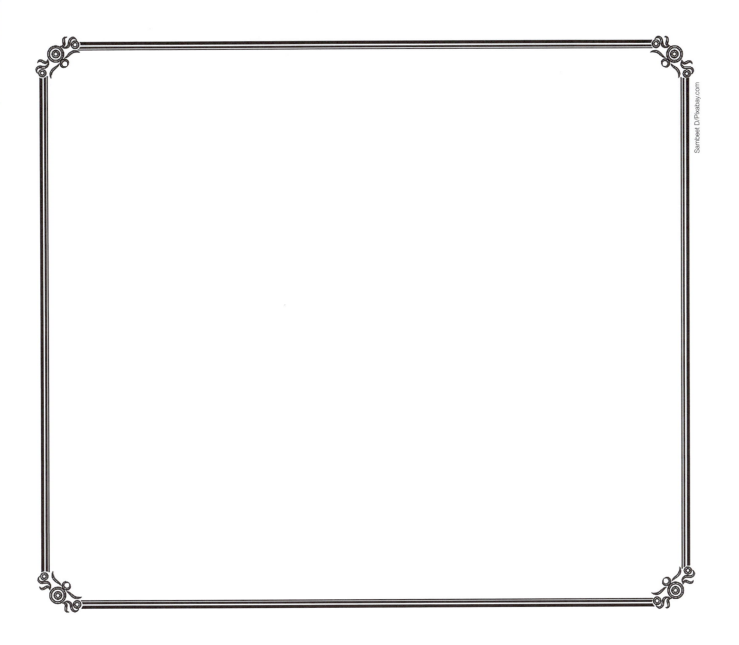

3 In pairs, introduce your relatives from the picture above to your classmate.

EXAMPLE

— Who is this?

— This is my aunt Anna.

— Who are these people?

— They are my sisters.

UNIT 5
MEANS OF TRANSPORTATION

1 Name the means of transportation.

a)

b)

c)

d)

e)

f)

g)

h)

i)

2 Draw the means of transportation into the correct categories.

Truck * Subway * Train
Hot-air ballon * Helicopter * Ship
Speedboat * Ferry * Plane

Land	Air	Water

UNIT 6
AT THE SCHOOL CAFETERIA

1 Name all the food items.

Cereal	Eggs	Bread	Pasta
Beans	Bacon	Mushrooms	Fruits
Tomatoes	Rice	Juice	Soup

2 Today we are going to grab a bite to eat at the school cafeteria. Read the menu and fill in the blanks with the words in the box.

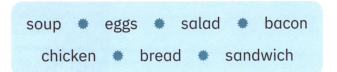

Today's Menu

Breakfast

a) Cheese _____

b) _____ and _____

c) _____

Lunch

d) _____

e) _____

f) _____

3 Read these school lunch menus around the world.

A lunch menu from a school in Nigeria

MONDAY	TUESDAY	WEDNESDAY	THURSDAY	FRIDAY
Rice Beans Beef Fruits	Spaghetti Chicken Fruits	Rice Chicken Vegetables Fruits	Potato Fish Fruits	Rice Salad Chicken Fruits

Available at: https://i.pinimg.com/736x/1f/0f/e8/1f0fe825e0ed7e99af89334a69429c85.jpg.
Access on: 23rd Feb. 2024.

A lunch menu from a school in England

MONDAY	TUESDAY	WEDNESDAY	THURSDAY	FRIDAY
Chicken Rice Banana cake	Cheese and broccoli spaghetti Strawberry	Mixed bean wrap Rice Ice cream	Chicken taco Rice Chocolate cookie	Cheese or tomato pasta Carrot cake

Available at: https://wytonprimaryschool.org.uk/SchoolLunches.htm.
Access on: 6th Mar. 2023

4 Compare the menus and tick the kind of food each school has.

	THE NIGERIAN SCHOOL	THE BRITISH SCHOOL
FRUITS		
PASTA		
CHICKEN		
FISH		
SWEETS		

5 Are these healthy menus?

_____

_____

6 Unscramble the letters to find a combination of food that Nigerians and Brazilians eat a lot: **IREC** and **SABNE**

_____ and _____

TWENTY-THREE 23

7 What do you eat in your school? Complete the sentence.

In my school I eat _____

_____

_____

_____

_____

8 Organize the food items in the table below. Then draw the food items.

Sugar ✸ Potatoes ✸ Cheese
Cookies ✸ Apples ✸ Eggs
Bread ✸ Milk ✸ Coffee ✸ Carrots

How many _____ are there?	How much _____ is there?
_____	_____
_____	_____
_____	_____
_____	_____

9 Complete the questions using **How many** or **How much**.

a) — _____ cupcakes are there in the box?

— There are 2 cupcakes in the box.

b) — _____ juice is there in the fridge?

— There is some juice in the fridge.

c) — _____ eggs do you need for the cake?

— I need 3 eggs.

d) — _____ sugar do you need?

— I need 2 bags of sugar.

UNIT 7
A MESSAGE TO A FRIEND

1 Rewrite the message below replacing the emojis with words.

Subject: The class party
Cc:
From: Elena (ElenaMacarty@email.com)
To: Carol (CarolKlinton@email.com)

Hey, Carol,

I am 😊 for the class party tomorrow.

What 🧥 are you wearing?

What ⌚ are you going to the party?

Can you ☎ me?

See you.

_____
_____
_____
_____
_____

2 What is the feeling?

a)

_____

b)

_____

c)

_____

d)

_____

e)

_____

f)

_____

3 Work in pairs. The teacher will give each one of you cards with emojis that represent different feelings. Show a flashcard to each other and make a sentence using the adjective that is represented by that specific emoji. Example: **Happy** – "I feel happy when I go to the beach."

How do you feel?

4 You are going to mime to represent a feeling and try to guess your classmates' mimes. With all the students in a circle, the teacher will choose, every round, one of you to mime while the others try to guess which feeling is being represented.

Miming Game

UNIT 8
TRAVELING WITH FRIENDS

1 Match the images to the activities.

a)

☐ To sunbathe

b)

☐ To play frisbee

c)

☐ To go sailing

d)

☐ To build sandcastles

30   THIRTY

2 Put the letters of the words in order to complete the dialogue between Justin and Anna.

Justin: — What a beautiful day! I love the _____! (EACBH)

Anna: — Me too, Justin! It's my favorite place to go on vacation! I'm crazy about playing _____! (EEFSBRI)

Justin: — I love it! And I love building _____! Let's build one! We can collect beautiful _____ to put on it! (DCANSATLESS/ESHAELLS)

Anna: — Good idea! But before that I want to _____. (UNSBHEAT)

Justin: — Ok! In the afternoon I am going _____ with my parents! Would you like to come? (SLINAIG)

Anna: — Yes! I'd love to!

3 Unscramble the sentences.

During vacation...

a) likes to / go to the theater / She
___

b) takes / He / of sculptures / photos
___

c) the bookstore / They / go to
___

d) do / I / crafts
___